THE

IDENTIFICATION

OF GHOSTS

THE
IDENTIFICATION
OF GHOSTS

Maryrose Larkin

chax press 2013

ISBN 978-0-9894316-4-4

Printed in USA

Published by Chax Press
411 N 7th Ave Ste 103
Tucson Arizona 85705-8388

Acknowledgement:

Parts of this work have appeared in *c_L, CLOCK, Peaches and Bats, Horse
Less Review, Trickhouse* and *Wheelhouse*. Special thanks to Eric Matchett,
the Spare Roomies, Anne Gorrick, Sarah Mangold, Catherine Daly, Jai Milx
and especially to the editors of Little Red Leaves, without whom this poem
would not exist.

for Bud Larkin

energy that when released can become damage

Saint black rabbit are your lungs a vessel or a fluster or
a ghost that resembles you & your halved eye blue as
chamber to clavicle

rabbit black were his symptoms questions waiting for
answers or 4 masked men in the house

passage or shimmer the porch light atlantic & human at
once the image   ghosts

even when we translated the madness or gesture as arrows &
        empires
the names as random trust in touch & hazard in
situation

rattle awake & object at sea or elsewhere facts decoding
where the meaning of the sentence indicates a rabbit's shape

a muse in a half shroud
one can be immortal

this perception is called a malfunction

mixed skull & shavings
pressed into the wall

survival is where
I read the into the storm hours all to almost

the word *no* is the prime opponent

Wander or where where one should not be

a rabbit
        risen at random

it hands move so as to escape
by chance or arrive somewhere

capacitance
 (of an animal)

having no or having wandered
of the eyes or by the mistake

only this far & still
survival is a cipher

even when translated

it occurs to people

distorted sometimes drastic
an astray out lived rite

Do you think the dead sound
more like sand or water?

the sentence apart

intention

under
gloss : I'm sounding
out the river
as forever

how your empire
assembled

saints wander into the house of line

cathedrals'
water & sand

drift as attribute
meaning sister

term
blurred notation
forward ghost

the   candle   &   the   drift

regarding sleep: a muse is buckled down in a room

one eye closed

almost morning & specifically is an outlived rite
sorrow cipher pitch

rising a variation
on to the next mistake

grief house
extends from the eye

illness gives way to rot &

an animal is mostly structures without citations
an index of despair rabbit back rabbit black prey

how I lost the wiki of how
one can be immortal &
human at once

but no one
how could one ever one
is more likely never to

his lungs at ninety
percent squamous

how I continued to believe

trust in touch & hazard in situation

the score in which the I structure
the word is it understood as a whole

moral panic is
a method of being awake

but most use the sleeping variation

as a specimen   of the eyes or   by the mistake

no infinite structure labeled The Canon

extends the eye
throughout illness

may you find
the sentence apart of
 a track along the sheath

it occurs to all

rattle & deficit
remorse white

fingers rattle
a tract along the sheath

he was born a ghost

intubate and

shroud
unwound &
fade

he bore it on his palm

This section is missing citations
an axe fell from the sky

decoding   dreamer
assigning cures
from the day's residue

schools of thought
discuss the process of meaning

ascribe the dream
        to part of the human   & part of the animal

rabbit black rabbit back pray dreaming
the patterns of the dark

 indication of the animal
You may have been shooting . May you find
intuition and grace

24

distorting heaven measure hour

saint ash palate

4 bodies in the house of bodies

violence inner in method an hour unwound or a

story unwound as how could one ever

only see death as an isolated event I always thought

I would be *saint barren & salt*

definition passage blossom & 13 vessels lost

consequence
embracing
 sight

I placed

the answers on a shelf in the storm the rabbit into the
sentence

saint of arrows & also
saint of the shadow of arrows
& of the shadows' shadows
saint root

he bore heart apocrypha shredded

clavicle moths
he bore wings erupting
lungs all shadow & no potentials

evoked as almost empire leaning in on the other side

only this far & still
I wanted to be a stray

falling from the sky
is closely identified as empire

steel eye description
remorse the rabbit ears held white against eve

constructed of an axe
the shadows of the arrows

     & of *the patterns of the dark*
sound a domain of ghosts

it occurs to many

& against the facts
denial with a path erupting beside it
but no holy c

no holy consequence

of the same kind
written as tragedy

or kept where other items
what is it good for having

no or having wandered
where a person suffers

scaped luna

spare us your most abundant
indications of the rabbit as forever

even when translated definition is a hollow where
we intubate the living & shroud the dead

 how I continued to believe in macular seas
metallic whites

the broken grist
is no boundary between 3 & one ghost

a vessel who was born as empty

over
the heart
suspended

petals in the hollowed out

of a rabbit) the upstairs window *which supports structural o*

measure
working curiosity discuss

saint invalid patterns against the dark

an axe fell

hearing a half turn a shimmer

fact becoming facets would be
pacific as an image

or an isolated event

a prime number for the questions or 4 bodies / 4 rabbits

may you find
how could one's eye ever out

senses latticed half black through illness a

wind o penance unseen hour a seam
embracing the absent & assigning cures

from one to the next mistake
an apple tree

slue rabbit caught & continually grieving
rite kindred & into empire

a name blossoms
under

predicting the connective & continual grief

anger when released can cause damage   to ghosts
measure the work now vanished

the saint of the arrow you may have been shooting

definition a   crook where we leave our
muse

eye as a central line and as a cathedral
These perceptions are called *entropic*

In a dark room with one eye closed move
means of rays and again fires vernacular

he was born a ghost

to the empty well bring the sea & the consequences

the workings of
empire outlived

her own devices are the opponent of heaven

as an apple tree loves
ravaged & fire white

as an apple tree moves
from one mistake to another

the candle &   the drift
one is more likely to

or 4 masked men
storm
into

or the body in action or
 preoccupation

or 4 bodies in
catch & into empire

 violence
or 4 bodies in

or 3 and one ghost

His symptoms shrouded

the madness of many
is empire specifically

there is no boundary between

for the questions
image as incident
or gesture as

abstractions are *the prime opponent of heaven*

too barren & salt

sparrow separates its wings into sentences
arrows & essential knowledge

sparrow gives way as a
 specimen wanderer or being awake & grace

saint citation
resassembled

rays &
an April diagnosis lead to

the body in action
or   a house of unnatural tracts

specifically
to dress
bone in
weather

transverse to
the workings
of empire

to fill
the broken grist
with sight

the wings (sparrow)
& the rabbit's body

is it the sound

or the meaning
wings' inner surface

that extends from the
mean to the

tip of the
infinite itself

inner surface
traversed

49

only translated
this far
white

abandoned to
to cipher

beginning the often

how I wanted to be either be astray
or kept where other items of the same kind are

house of
hours

house of
arrow arrow

house of

unseen
sparrow

house of
sorrow

empires vary
from basically all to almost no

sentence as sense as a structure named *The Canon*

balance predicting
malfunction

how it works in
bone ravaged
moth latticed
broken

what is this weeping good for
is there something you'd like to add

remorse a metallic white held against fragmentation
to part of the human saint of the arrow & also saint of
drift as

this emerging sense of what I lost

a wholly a secondary mixed & shavings
redwing August & his symptoms sung

nature loves crisis   as an apple tree loves apples loves automobiles rabbit & sparrow

written as a tragedy
how she wanted to be astray

escaped saint of the arrow
escape moon

do the dead sound out the river

but no one trust in touch & hazard

having no or having wandered

may you find

Maryrose Larkin lives in Portland, Oregon. She is the author of *Inverse, The Whimsy Daybook, The Book of Ocean, The Name of this Intersection is Frost,* and *Marrowing.* Her most recent project *Speaking Buildings* transects the constraints of windows and history.

Chax Press is a 501(c)(3) nonprofit organization, founded in 1984, and has published more than 150 books, including fine art and trade editions of literature and book arts works.

For more information, please see our web site at http://chax.org

Chax Press is supported by individual contributions, and by the Tucson Pima Arts Council and the Arizona Commision on the Arts, with funds from the State of Arizona and the National Endowment for the Arts.